W9-AJS-320

And Other Annoying (but True) Life Lessons

by Marc Gellman

Illustrated by Debbie Tilley

LITTLE, BROWN AND COMPANY
New York Boston

To my mother Rosalie — This is the day I thank you for this.

Little, Brown and Company

Hachette Book Group USA
237 Park Avenue, New York, NY 10169
Visit our Web site at www.lb-kids.com

First Edition: May 2007

Library of Congress Cataloging-in-Publication Data

Gellman, Marc.
Someday you'll thank me for this! : and other annoying (but true) life lessons / by Marc Gellman ; illustrated by Debbie Tilley — 1st ed.
p. cm.
ISBN-13: 978-0-316-01234-8
ISBN-10: 0-316-01234-3
1. Parent and child — Juvenile literature. 2. Child rearing — Juvenile literature.
I. Tilley, Debbie. II. Title.
HQ772.5.G457 2007
306.874 — dc22

2006032235

10 9 8 7 6 5 4 3 2 1

Q-FF

Printed in the United States of America

Contents

From the Author: How to Speak Parent

When I was a kid, I thought the only reason I had a middle name was to help my parents tell me I was in deep trouble. When they yelled, "Marc *Alan* Gellman, *come down here right now*!" I knew my life was basically over and that I was about to be grounded forever. Sometimes, as I was going to my room to serve my time, my mom or my dad would say, "Someday you'll thank me for this!" I remember thinking, "You're *punishing* me. Don't expect me to *thank* you for it!" It seemed totally stupid to thank them on the day I got punished, and I definitely had no plans to thank them on any other day.

What I now understand is that even though I could hear what they were saying, I couldn't understand what they *meant*—probably because I didn't have a book like this one. Parents and kids speak different languages, and this book teaches kids something I had a hard time figuring out: how to speak and understand the secret language of Parent.

Parent is a language that sounds like English (or Spanish or any other language your parents speak). But it's not really English at all. It's a secret language spoken only by parents. Parents speak this language mostly when they're telling you to do something or not do something. You hear the words they're saying, but you don't hear the secret meaning behind those words. The secret meaning is what your parents *really* mean when they tell you what to do.

The thing is, the annoying stuff your parents and grandparents and teachers and coaches (and sometimes your friends) tell you all the time are annoying for two reasons: 1) you hear them over and over again, and 2) they seem to be about such little things, you can't even believe you're being nagged about them.

If you spoke Parent, though, you'd understand that these little things only seem to be little things, but they all have a bigger, deeper meaning hiding underneath. They're sort of like Tootsie Pops: the little meaning of the saying is like the hard candy coating, and the big meaning is like the chewy center. You can't get to the big meaning until you lick off the candy coating, which you can only do if you speak Parent.

You'll probably understand how to speak Parent someday if you have children. It seems to come naturally with the territory when you become a parent. The problem is that if you can't translate Parent into English right now, you'll probably get in trouble. This is a major pain for you as a kid, and it doesn't need to happen. Once you speak Parent, you can understand the meaning behind the meaning of what your parents nag you about all the time. Like most things in life that seem complicated, it's all really very simple.

This book is like a "get-out-of-jail-free" card to use with your parents. In some board games, if you have that card and you land in jail, you can just use the card to keep going without losing a turn or paying any money. The way I see it, if this book can keep you from having your life as you know it ruined by being grounded until you're old, it's a good thing.

This book will also help you remember that despite how clueless your parents seem to you at times, they have two big things going for them: they love you, and they know more than you do.

Most of the people you meet have no idea who you

are. Some people know you. Some people know you and like you. And some people know you and love you, and those are the people you can trust the most in your life. And when people who know you *and* love you tell you something, you can trust that they're not telling you stuff just to get you to go away or to make your life miserable; it's almost always because they love you. Speaking in Parent is one of the main ways they show their love.

As much as you hate to admit it, your parents do know some stuff you don't because they've lived longer. The word for that is *wisdom*. Wisdom is knowing what really matters in life. Being wise is not like being smart. You can be smart even when you are very young. For example, some kids can play chess or add numbers or read or play musical instruments really well when they're very young because they're very smart or gifted with certain abilities, but you cannot be wise when you are young. You need time to become wise and your parents have had time. When they tell you something, it's usually because they've faced what you're facing now and they learned from it.

Wisdom is kind of like being able to look around the corner to see what's there. Listening to your parents allows you to look around the corners of life. That's a good thing to be able to do, and that's the second reason why you'll want to learn to understand Parent.

I hope this book starts up some good conversations with your parents about what really matters in life. I hope it gets you to trust them more, and I hope it gets them to trust you more. I hope, most of all, that you have a great life and that someday you might have children who also have no idea what you are talking about — until they learn to speak Parent, too!

So, trust me; someday you'll thank me for this.

1

Someday you'll thank me for this!

For some strange reason, a lot of the most annoying things you get told all the time by your parents begin with "Some-day . . ." I guess "Someday" is a big word in the language of Parent! And "Someday you'll thank me for this" is usually dished out by your parents after they ground you or bring down some other cruel and unusual punishment on your innocent head. It's a real double whammy because not only are you being punished, but someday you're supposed to be *thankful* that you were punished!

The thing is, someday you'll have to protect yourself because your parents won't be around, but right now it's one of your parents' biggest jobs to protect you, even when you don't think you need protecting — and even when you don't *want* to be protected.

Maybe you get into an argument with your folks over going to a party where there are no parents in the house or maybe they'll refuse to take you to a movie that they think you're too young to see. This may be really upsetting to you, particularly if your friends' parents let them do something that your folks won't let you do.

Your parents are kind of like your life umpires, as long as you live in their house. And just like baseball and football, sometimes the umpires blow a call, but usually they get it right. It's the same with parents. When parents are wrong, well, then all you've lost is one good time (and you might have missed one lame party), but when they're right, they might actually have saved your life.

If you made a list of all the things your parents need to do for you (like get you to school on time and feed you real food and buy you clothes that cover your body), it would be a long list, but if you add to that list the things they don't need to do for you but do anyway (like buying you a video-game controller, or an iPod, or a cell phone; or putting an ice-cream factory in the basement, a swimming pool in your bedroom, or a pet horse in your living room), that list (okay, I got a little carried away with the list) would be so long you couldn't even write it all down. And after they do all of those things for you, your parents don't even ask you to thank them.

But someday far in the future, when you realize that your parents helped teach you a big life lesson that might have hurt at the time, you should call them up and say, "You know how when I wanted to put a swimming pool in my bedroom, but you said NO! and I freaked out and you said, 'Someday you'll thank me for this'? Well, I just wanted to call you and tell you that today was the day. I just put a swimming pool in my bedroom and the cat almost drowned and all my clothes are wet and the floating duck keeps me up at night. Anyway, I just wanted to thank you!"

It's amazing how, "Someday you'll thank me for this" could really mean *today*. If you thank your parents not only for what they do for you but also for what they keep you from doing, it will make their day. And it's a fair trade — because they made your life.

2

To be a dessert something has to be sweet and delicious, or crunchy or cold, or topped with whipped cream, or drizzled with chocolate or marshmallow sauce, or squashed between two cookies, or baked between two pie-crusts, or covered with sprinkles, or baked into a frosted cake, or filled with jelly, or topped with powdered sugar, or covered with fruit, or piled on a plate with other cookies.

And dessert can never *ever* be green, unless it's lime Jell-O, which is barely a dessert anyway. (After all, it's what they serve you for dessert when you're in the hospital, and hospitals are clueless about dessert!)

Dessert isn't just what you eat last, either. If you eat

asparagus last at your next meal, asparagus wouldn't be dessert — it would just be the green veggies you ate at the wrong time.

So think about those days when you come home to the smell of freshly baked cookies; and you look around; and there is nobody in the kitchen except you and those warm, gooey, delicious cookies; and you sneak up to the cookies very quietly so that your sneakers won't squeak on the kitchen floor; and you reach out your trembling hand to grab the goods; and then suddenly — as if by magic — the cookie police swoops down and stops you, cookie-less and drooling, by shouting, "The cookies are just for dessert!"

Basically, dessert is a bribe. We eat it last because if we were allowed to eat it first, we wouldn't eat anything else.

Every kid knows this, and every parent knows this. And when kids grow up and turn into parents, they know this. This is why your folks are always trying to keep you away from the dessert until you finish your nasty asparagus. Besides, you really can't live on a diet of cookies, even if you have them with milk.

This whole thing isn't only about cookies. The cookie saying is really about learning to control your appetites. You've heard of your *appetite* — the thing that kicks in when your stomach starts growling loudly as you wait for the lunch bell to ring — but you will have many kinds of appetites in your life. They're the things your body or your mind makes you crave, like candy bars or fancy electronics or cool friends. Appetites are not bad if you control them. They're bad if they control you.

Hunger is the first appetite you have in life. Some people can't control their eating, so they eat even when they're not hungry. They let their eating control them rather than controlling their appetite. Wanting stuff like a new iPod or sneakers is an appetite, too. We see things we want but don't have, and that makes us want to buy, buy, buy.

The problem is, when all you think about is having more things, you can't enjoy the things you already have. The truth is, stuff — even really cool stuff — can't make you happy for very long; only surrounding yourself with good people and doing good things can. I took a rich kid I know to a place where poor hungry people go to eat lunch for free. It's called a soup kitchen. That day a little girl named Maria came through the line, and when she got to the dessert she smiled and started to cry. There was a birthday cake with "Happy Birthday" written on top in red icing. The baker had given the cake to the soup kitchen because the person who ordered it never came by to pick it up. The rich kid asked the little girl why she was crying and she said, "How did you know it was my birthday today?" She never had a birthday cake before because she was so poor.

After that day, the rich kid started to give away some of his stuff and spend more time doing good things, like going to soup kitchens. That day he learned that stuff does not make you happy. Doing kind things makes you happy.

Remember: it's not only great to end your meals with something good and sweet like cookies, but *everything* you do should end with something sweet. When you end a letter or an e-mail, I hope you end it with something sweet and kind like, "Hope to see you soon" or "You're the best!" When you leave your friend's house, I hope you don't forget to thank your friend's parents for letting you come to visit. Those are all "cookie things," even if they don't have anything to do with cookies.

So, think about cookie things, and every ending will be a little bit sweeter. That's the reason for dessert; that's the reason for cookies; and that's the real translation from Parent into English of "The cookies are just for dessert!"

3

I don't know about you, but I always liked my room messy. I liked knowing that my dirty underwear was on the bed-post, right where it could dry out and I could wear it again. I liked leaving cold, half-eaten pizza slices under my bed, right where I could grab them for breakfast. I liked having my bats and balls on the floor near the door so that my sister would trip over them if she tried to sneak into my room and take my cool stuff. Most of all, I liked the idea that in my room I could put (or throw) my things where I wanted them to be put (or thrown). My stuff, my room, my way: it just seemed right to me.

Unfortunately, it did not seem right to my mom, who had other ideas. The irritating parent saying I heard most was definitely, “Clean up your room!” I never understood why my mom had such an interest in my private space and in my underwear-cold-pizza-sister-trap filing system. I put a “GO AWAY!” sign on the outside of my bedroom door to scare my mom away, but you can’t scare moms away. And when you’re a kid, nobody respects your signs anyway.

Then, one day I was over at my friend Craig’s house, and I saw him do something I had never ever seen any one of my friends do before. Before we went out to play baseball, Craig put his dirty clothes in a laundry basket AND carried his dirty laundry downstairs. And then he put his laundry in the washing machine, AND he turned it on. I looked at him like he had two heads, and he said, “What? I do this all the time. It’s no big deal.”

But then the most amazing part happened: Craig's mom came in and said, "You're the best, Craigy. I really needed that today."

When I got home later that day something deep inside me decided that I wanted my mom to be proud of me, too. So, that day I ate all the pizza under my bed (yes, I did get sick). I took my underwear off the bedpost and disconnected my baseball-bat-sister trap. I cleaned up my room without being asked, and I kept it mostly clean and pizza-free until I moved out. (Then, it got messy again, but that's another story.)

That day at Craig's, I finally figured out that my room wasn't really *my* room. It was my room in my parents' house. My parents worked hard to make a home for us, and by keeping my room full of crud I was saying that I didn't respect how hard they were working to make it a nice place to live. "Clean up your room" wasn't about cold pizza under my bed. It was about being a part of a family and doing my part to make our family work.

You know when somebody isn't respecting you, but do you really know when you're not respecting somebody else? Respect has to go both ways for it to be real. If it only comes from others, that's not fair. That's the deal, and cleaning your room is part of the deal.

Now, if you happen to have a housekeeper or cleaning person who makes the beds and does the laundry, that doesn't get you off the clean-room hook. If you keep your room clean and bring down your dirty laundry, then the cleaning people don't have to do that for you, and they can clean other parts of the house instead of your room. Then, they can finish faster and save your parents some money.

By doing your part, you're showing that you respect your family, even if it means giving up having cold pizza and used underwear close by at all times. Believe me, hot pizza, clean underwear, and happy parents are all worth it.

4

Turn off the lights when you leave the room!

You may be a small person, but you're a part of a big world, and that world needs your help. It's getting hot and dirty, and it needs you and me and everybody living here on planet Earth to help make it cool and clean again. That's what your parents are trying to teach when they nag you with what seems to be a very nitpicky message: "Turn off the lights when you leave the room!"

If you think they're just yapping about one measly lightbulb, you may get upset at them for making such a big deal about nothing. I know and you know that turning out the lights in one room in one house in one state in one country on one continent isn't going to clean up the whole entire earth, but you would be surprised to learn how much it matters if we *all* do it.

Did you know it costs about fifty cents to buy enough electricity to run one 100-watt lightbulb for one month? But nobody just leaves one light on when they leave the room. If you turn eight lights on in your house for a month, it could cost your parents about four dollars. Now let's say that half the time those lights are on, you're not even in the room. That means that you're wasting about two dollars a month on lighting up rooms with nobody in them.

And that's just for the lights! Many people also leave the TV on when they leave the room, and it costs about four dollars to run a TV eight hours a day for a month. So, if you're not watching the TV for half that time, you can add another two dollars to the wasted electricity pile which is now up to four dollars of wasted electricity a month.

Don't worry, my math problem is almost over. The really mind-blowing stuff is still to come! Listen to this: How would you like it if I gave you forty-eight dollars so that you could buy forty-eight songs for your iPod or three DVDs? All of that wasted electricity adds up to forty-eight dollars a year in money wasted on lighting rooms with no one in them, and showing TV programs to no one, except maybe your dog or cat or fish or hamster — and let me tell you, hamsters do not really like to watch that much TV! (Well, that's not completely true. There is a new show called *The World Hamster Wrestling Federation*, which hamsters just love, but if you watch this show with your hamster, then you're not *really* wasting electricity.)

Saving your family forty-eight dollars a year is just the beginning of the good things you're doing by turning out the lights when you leave the room. Let's imagine that there are about 1 million homes in America. If each home saved forty-eight dollars a year by turning off the lights, America could save 48 million dollars a year! Now 48 million dollars is real money, and that money could be used to give food to poor people or to take care of cats and dogs that no-

body wants. Turning off the lights turns on all those good things.

You see, when you turn on the light switch or press the power button on the TV remote control, you're sending a signal through electrical wires to a place called a transmission station. The transmission station gets its electricity from big engines at a power plant that need fuel to run, and that fuel usually comes from gas, oil, or coal. Burning fuel creates a lot of gases that come out of tall smokestacks and spread out like a blanket over the earth. This blanket makes the earth a little warmer than it should be. These warmer temperatures are melting ice at the North and South Poles, which could raise the level of Earth's oceans. And some places that are very close to the level of the oceans, like Florida, might get flooded.

This is part of a big environmental change called global warming, and you'll learn a lot of scary things about it in school. But what your teacher might not say is this: If Florida gets flooded one day, what if some old golfers get stuck out there floating around on their golf carts? Since golf carts don't float too well, they'll be in big trouble. The chances are that one or two or maybe three or four of these old golfers in Florida are your grandparents. So turn off the lights when you leave a room so that your grandparents can play golf without having to be rescued from the hot-dog stand on the ninth hole!

Of course, global warming is not just bad for golfers. The hurricanes and the droughts and much of the really bad weather we are experiencing may be coming from all the gases we put in the air when we drive our cars and the electricity we use to light the rooms that we're not even in! It would be a bad thing to wake up one day and hear that the Statue of Liberty is up to her waist in water, and that polar bears can't survive because there is no ice left for them to walk on, and that the African deserts are getting even bigger. Even though some of these changes may take hundreds or thousands of years to happen, we need to try to fix this problem now before things get worse.

The main thing to remember is that *every little thing you do really does matter*. You may think that you're just a part of your family, but you're really a part of a big country and an even bigger world. If you ever go to the Grand Canyon, in Arizona, you can see how little things make a big difference. That huge canyon was carved out of the rocks in the desert by tiny drops of water that flowed together to make small streams that flowed together to make big rivers that cut through the rock over thousands of years and dug out the Grand Canyon.

You're just one of about six billion people who live on planet Earth. If we work together, though, everything on Earth could be cleaner — and the most amazing thing is that all of this could start just by flipping a little switch! Every person on planet Earth will be proud of you — except of course, your hamster, who would be much happier running on his wheel while watching hamster wrestling on TV.

5

"Time-out!" sounds like it's nothing, but you know the truth: Time-outs are kind of like being thrown into jail by your parents — except there are no bars on the windows and you don't get a fancy lawyer to argue your case.

I'm sure I don't have to explain time-outs to you, but for the one person on the planet who doesn't know, a time-out is when you get sent to the corner or to your room as punishment for something you probably think is minor — like having a who-can-spit-the-farthest contest with your brother — but drives your parents so crazy that it seems they just can't stand to see or talk to you for a little while.

When you're a bit older but still living at home, it isn't

called a time-out anymore — it's probably called "being grounded." Older kids often call it "being busted" or if it's very bad, they call it "being SO busted." Whatever you or your parents call it, time-outs are a kind of punishment.

You may think that punishments are *always* bad, but I think time-outs are punishments that can turn out to be good. They give you a chance to calm down, relax, and get control of yourself. You know how after you run, you need time to catch your breath? Well, that's what a time-out allows you to do: catch your breath. A time-out is like a commercial break from an argument, and it gives everyone time to think. Afterwards, you're cooler, and (hopefully) so are they.

Nobody likes to be ordered around, and when you're a kid you get ordered around a lot. I know how it is — sometimes you just lose control because you want to do something you can't, like skateboard at dinnertime or watch someone on television swallow ten creepy-crawly bugs without puking while you're supposed to be doing your homework. Or you don't want to do something you have to do, like clear everyone else's mess from the kitchen table. So, some days you might just snap and scream, "LEAVE ME ALONE!" Well, then, a time-out is just what you wanted. It's time for people to leave you alone.

And I'll tell you a secret your parents might not want me to reveal: sometimes, even the people who take care of you need some quiet time away from you. They still love you, but they can get fed up with you just like you can get fed up with them. And who knows? Once in a great while, they might need your time-out to understand that maybe they're pushing you too hard, or ordering you around just a little too much. So, even if you're never given a time-out, you may decide that you need to give yourself your own time-outs.

Some people take time-outs by going out for a run or a long walk and listening to the birds in the trees or to the wind blow. Some people take a time-out by painting or writing poetry. Some people take time-outs when they meditate, which is a way to clear your mind of all thoughts and emotions. Some people take time-outs when they pray. Some people take time-outs before they fall asleep by thinking about their day and about what they did to help or hurt people.

People who take their own time-outs can think about what they love and give thanks for what they have. They begin to really understand what matters and what doesn't matter in their lives. They think about forgiving people who have hurt them, and they think about ways to do good and live meaningful lives.

With too much quiet time you can go nuts, but with too little quiet time you can become lost. So the next time you are grounded or sent for a time-out, you can really freak your folks out if, instead of yelling and screaming, "I hate you!" or "That's not fffffaaaaiiiirrr!!!" you just smile, look at them, and say, "Thanks. I needed that."

6

Would you rather eat ice cream or liver and onions? Would you rather go to a ball game and get hot dogs and popcorn or go to the dentist and have your teeth drilled? These are the easy choices, but in life you also have to make tough choices like whether you'll play fair or cheat.

It's too bad that there are just so many ways to cheat. Most sports don't have umpires or line judges, so you have to trust the other players and they have to trust you. In tennis you can cheat by calling a ball out when it's really in. In soccer you can trip other players to keep them from getting to the ball. In baseball you can throw the ball at another player's head. In cards you can try to sneak a peek at the other players' cards. In Scrabble you can look up the spelling of words you don't even know — words like QWERTY (which, by the way, means a standard arrangement of keys for the alphabet characters on a computer keyboard). And, of course, in tiddlywinks you can cheat by hiding the other player's winks!

You know the right thing to do, but you just want to win so badly that you might choose to cheat just to get what you want and to get it now! Making this bad choice once makes it easier to decide to cheat again and again. Pretty soon, you might just forget what it means to play fair.

What makes the choice to play fair so hard is that when you're playing a cheater, the cheaters often win. You might have seen news stories about major league baseball players,

pro football players, and track runners who took drugs called steroids. These drugs might have made the athletes stronger so they could hit more home runs, pitch better, and run faster in the short term, but the steroids may have also had bad effects on their health. What's even worse is that after seeing famous athletes use steroids, some high school athletes started copying them. When you cheat, it isn't just bad for you — it could set a bad example for other people.

Besides, winning by cheating takes all the fun out of winning. Even if nobody but you knows that you cheated, *you* still know, and it makes the victory very hollow. It's like eating and never getting full. It's like having a birthday party and never smiling. The only way to be proud of winning is to win fair and square. (By the way, why do they say "fair and square"? Why don't they say fair and round or fair and purple? It makes no sense.)

In life, one thing always leads to another — it's a law of life, like the law that everything that tastes good has too much sugar and everything that's good for you tastes like celery. Remember that cheating in sports will teach you to cheat in other areas of your life — like school. Cheating on tests is much easier if you're already a cheater in sports.

Playing fair is more fun than cheating anyway. I once

met Sarah Hughes right after she won the women's Olympic gold medal in figure skating. I asked her which was more fun, the skating or the winning. She answered me fast, "The skating!" I told her, "That is why you won." When you play just to win, you can win or you can lose. When you play fair just for fun, you can never ever lose.

Only you can make the tough choice, and what you choose will change you and it might also change the people who admire you. Your parents believe in you. Your coaches believe in you. Your teachers believe in you. And I believe in you. So, if you try not to disappoint the people who believe in you, then you'll win every really important game you ever play.

7

Speak up so that Grandma and Grandpa can hear you!

When is a person old? When I was little, I thought people in college were old. Then, when I got to college, I thought people who were married were old. Then, when I got married, I thought that people who had kids were old. Then, when I had kids, I thought that people who had grandchildren were old. Now that I have grandchildren (Zeke and Daisy), the only people I think are old are the ones who can't smile anymore.

There are good and bad things about growing old. Some of the good things about growing old are that you get free coffee in some burger places and you get into movies for a cheaper price than everyone else does. There are also certain things about life that you just can't figure out until you're old — like what you're really good at, who really loves you, and what really matters to you in your life. The very best thing about growing old is that if you're lucky, you get to see the children of your children. And if you're very lucky, you get to see the children of your children's children.

Some bad things about growing old are that you can't hear, run, or jump the way you used to when you were younger. When you get old, your body starts to kind of fall apart, and you seem to have more pee and more gas. You have weaker muscles and weaker bones, and your face has more wrinkles in it (unless you get them erased with those new chemicals they have now). When you're old, it can be harder to remember things and harder to hear things. You can pretend to remember, and you can pretend to hear, but even that doesn't really work sometimes because you can forget what you're trying to pretend to remember or to hear.

Of course, some grandparents are not that old and can run and walk and hear you just fine. But the reason you should speak louder to grandparents who can't hear that well isn't just about grandparents and it's not just about old people either. The translation from Parent into English of, "Speak up so that Grandpa and Grandma can hear you" is something like this: "You should always try to understand the problems other people have and help them if you can."

A disability is something that makes it harder —but not necessarily impossible — for someone to do something like read a book or run in a race. There are all different kinds of disabilities, and people with disabilities sometimes need extra help. If you can help them, you should. After all, we all need help sometimes. That's what your parents are trying to teach you in the language of Parent when they tell you to speak up so that Grandma and Grandpa can hear you. They're hoping that next time, they won't even have to remind you to talk louder because you'll see your grandparents' disabilities and you'll *want* to help them.

Being sensitive to people with disabilities isn't only a way to help them, it's also a way to help you. By helping people who need help you become more kind, more caring, and more sensitive. You become a better person. The word for knowing when people need help is *compassion*. Talking louder to hard of hearing grandparents is a way to show compassion to people you really love and who really love you.

Helping people in need also helps you see the parts of you that need help. Every single one of us is disabled in some way. Maybe you have trouble with math, or you're afraid to speak in front of lots of people. No one's perfect. By helping other people deal with their broken parts, you may find yourself more willing to try to overcome your own broken parts.

I had an operation on my chest when I was fourteen, and it left a scar on my chest. I was so embarrassed by that scar that I became shy about it. Nobody understood how I felt, until I met somebody else who also had a scar on her chest, too. She knew what it was like to feel uncomfortable with how your body looks, and she helped me to get over it.

There's an old saying that states that to really understand a person you need to walk in his or her shoes. This means that we all need to try to understand what makes life hard for other people and to try to make it less difficult for them. I once heard a grandpa give this blessing to his grandson: "Listen to me," he said, looking into the eyes of his grandson. "In your life you're going to meet people who need help. If you can help them, help them."

I've heard many speeches and many blessings in my life, but that one was the very best.

8

The world is full of slime. There's that green slime that covers ponds in the summer. There's the slime that comes off frogs and fish and drips off your fingers and onto your feet when you hold them. There's the slime that clogs up the pipes in your house that's made up of hair and old toothpaste and everything else you drop down the drain.

Yes, it's true, I'm a kind of slime-ologist, and in all of my investigations, I can tell you that the worst kind of slime is word-slime. Word-slime is the gross stuff that comes out of your mouth when you curse. Imagine what you would look like with snot-colored slime oozing out of your mouth! So, when your parents or teachers or the people who love you say, "Don't you use that language with me!" they're trying to help you by telling you how gross and offensive you look.

When we swear we're really covering *other* people with word-slime, too. Word-sliming the people you don't like isn't any better than word-sliming the people you do like. Word-sliming is like hitting. You throw word-slime at the person you hate and then they throw it right back at you. Then what? Probably fighting.

Like when somebody spills the green mystery meat in the cafeteria on your clean clothes and then instead of acting sorry, he just laughs at how gross you look. So you stand up and throw pie in his face. Then, he word-slimes you and you word-slime him, and the next thing you know, you're

both in trouble with the principal — and you both have clothes that smell like bad food. Really, the whole fight started with word-slime and not with spilled mystery meat. Word-slime is like throwing gasoline on a fire. Word-slime makes everything go from bad to worse really fast.

Beware! Word-slime is ready to invade your world like creepy aliens from Mars. The school bus, cafeteria, and playground are all breeding grounds for icky slime, so make sure you're armed with protection. The best protection against using word-slime or getting into a fight because somebody else word-slimed you is to say this sentence over and over in your mind, "IT JUST DOESN'T MATTER!" It just doesn't matter what some mean person says to you, and it just doesn't matter why some people get angry at stupid little things. What matters is that you remember that none of this really matters. Remembering this calms you down and dries up the word-slime that's about to ooze out of your mouth and stink up your life.

When I grew up, if you were caught swearing, the adult who caught you might wash your mouth out with soap. Nowadays that's a little bit more difficult. Rappers and other pop stars often swear in their songs and in interviews. Characters in movies and TV shows use curse words a lot. Lots of famous people are sliming up their language in public nowadays. This does not make it right. Slime is still slime even if the slimer is famous.

Word-slime is replacing words. If you grow up cursing, you can forget about learning to communicate. Just like slime covers up what something really is, word-slime covers up what you really mean. Cursing is a way of destroying language.

If we curse, we don't really use words; we replace them with slime, which is like replacing talking with grunting. If you're angry at someone, the best way to deal with it is to learn how to put that anger into words that not only express your anger, but also explain it. Anger can be like acid. It eats through all your good parts and leaves behind nothing but slime. And using word-slime to express it is like hitting yourself on the head and expecting somebody else's head to hurt. So, if you just take a deep breath the next time you're angry, maybe you won't even need words. Learning how to control your anger will help you to express your anger in non-slimy words.

Your words paint a picture of how you want people to treat you. So if you want people to think that you're a creepy alien from Mars, well then, slime away, but if you want people to respect you, why not start with getting them to respect your words? Our hands and eyes and ears are our best way to touch the world, but our words are our best way to touch each other.

Try to reach out and touch someone without leaving any word-slime behind and you'll see what a joy it is to live a slime-free life!

9

Is there anything you want to tell me?

Our world is full of warning signs. It's just that some are easier to spot than others. There are stop signs that warn you to stop before you go forward. There are signs that warn you to look out for deer or ducks or bears crossing the road. One of the most important warning signs you'll ever see in your life isn't on any stick and not on any road. This is the warning sign you get when your folks or the people who take care of you ask this simple but really scary question: "Is there anything you want to tell me?"

That message is like a big sign that says, "*You're about to be grounded for the rest of your life because of something bad you did. BUT, because I love you, I'm going to give you just one last chance to confess. You will still get punished, but it won't be nearly as bad as it will be if you deny everything. If you play dumb and don't tell me, you will be so busted, you will be so grounded, you will be so toast that your life as you know it now will be totally over!"* Since all of that would never fit on any sign, your parents give you the short version of the confess-or-else warning.

This final warning is a way of giving you a last chance to make a good choice. Either you can tell your parents what you did and beg for mercy, or you can try to lie your way out of it. Lying might work, but it has three problems: 1) it's wrong, and 2) when the truth comes out, the punishment

is worse than if you had just told the truth in the first place, and 3) it ruins the trust your parents have in you.

Besides, what your parents are asking you goes way beyond finding out what you did (which they already know). They're really asking you, "Do you trust us?" The biggest part of love is trust. They're asking you if you trust them enough to come to them when you're scared or caught in a bad situation. They need to know that you can come to them with any problem you have, and you need to know that, too.

Even though it may not seem like it sometimes, your parents are on your side. They know that everybody messes up sometimes. The difference between people who keep messing up and people who learn from their mistakes is that the second group asks for help from the people they love and trust. Your parents want to help you work through your problems and come out a better person. When you're able to trust them, it will make you feel better even if you're telling them about something bad that you did. You won't feel alone; you will feel *bundled*.

Take one pencil and break it. It's easy, isn't it? Now take three pencils and hold them tightly together and try to break the three of them. You can't do it. That's what it means to be bundled. A tribe in Africa called the Masai have a saying, "Sticks in a bundle are unbreakable. Sticks alone can be broken by a child."

What's true for sticks is true for people. Your problems might be too much for you to handle alone, but when you're bundled together with people who love you, you're unbreakable.

10

Hey, you're no dummy: You already know that hanging your sister's favorite teddy bear in the shower and turning on the water is wrong. You already know that dressing up like a gorilla and jumping out of the closet when your little brother or sister is trying to go to sleep is wrong. You already know that writing "MS. SHLUMPWASSER IS A GEEK!" on your teacher's blackboard when she is out of the room is wrong. You already know that pulling a booger out of your nose and sticking it under your seat is wrong.

You know that a long list of things you do are wrong, but there is an even longer list of wrong things you do that you might not even know are wrong. Did you know that it's NOT okay to download music from the Internet without paying for it (unless the music is supposed to be free)? Did you know that it's NOT okay to copy something off the Internet and use it in your homework without telling your teacher where you got it?

One of those wrong things you may not know is wrong is interrupting. When I was your age, I would be sitting at dinner, and when I was done eating my green-bean casserole with the little fried onions on top (actually, I fed half of it to our dog, Heidi, when nobody was looking because it looked gross and tasted gross), I wanted to leave the table right away. So, in the middle of everyone's conversation I just blurted out, "Can I leave the table now?" I thought it was actually pretty nice of me to even ask.

You know how boring it can be to listen to adults talking about something you either don't understand or don't care about at all, like when they talk about where to buy the best fruit or what is happening in Outer Mongolia or what day they want to make an appointment for you to go to the dentist! When they talk about that kind of boring stuff, you want to just get out of there and do absolutely anything else — immediately. Some adult conversations are such snooze-fests that you'd rather do math homework than sit there and listen to them talk about things you couldn't care less about.

You don't have that many ways to break free of boring adult conversations, so your best move is to just wait for a break in the conversation and then politely ask, "May I please be excused from your boring conversation so I can go do my math homework?" This usually works, because frankly, they probably don't really want you there anyway. (I just hope that you don't come from a family where people talk so much that you have to wait until breakfast the next day for everyone to stop talking.)

You may think that compared to giving your little sister's favorite stuffed animal to your dog as a chew toy,

feeding your brother's goldfish a slice of pizza, or hiding in your sister's closet and listening to her talk to her boyfriend, interrupting does not deserve to be anywhere on the list of the really bad things you did this week.

But here's the thing: interrupting tells people you think you're more important than they are. It's not just impolite to interrupt. Impolite is when you belch or pass gas or sneeze without covering your mouth. Wrong is when you don't listen to other people, because it says, "I don't care." There is no way to listen to what other people are saying if you're always interrupting.

Not waiting for a person to finish a sentence is like telling someone to get out of your way because you're more important than anyone else here on planet Earth. It's like beeping a horn at the car in front of you or cutting in line ahead of all the other people who are waiting their turn.

When you're on a long car trip and you tell your folks you need to stop for a bathroom break, you want people to listen to you, right? You wouldn't be too happy if your mom interrupted your potty plea with, "Oh, honey, can you turn up the radio? I love this song."

The truth is that nobody is more important than anyone else. All people you meet in your life deserve the same kind of respect, and that respect begins by letting them finish what they're saying before you say what's on your mind.

You're going to be on lots of teams in your life. Sometimes you'll be the team leader, and when you are, you'll learn that people don't follow a leader who doesn't listen to them. Great leaders come in all shapes and sizes, but they all have one quality in common: they're all great listeners.

If you've ever had a great coach, you know that the best coaches are often not the ones who know the game the best; they're the ones who know their players the best. And the reason they know their players is that they're good listeners and they don't interrupt. If you ever had a great teacher, you know that the best teachers are not the ones who know the most but the ones who can listen the best to your questions and then answer them. If you ever worked on a project at school, you know that the kids who get things done are not the ones who talk the most but the ones who listen and help others work together.

You may think that interrupting will get you what you want, but it won't get you what you need. What you need is to learn from the people who love you, and you can't learn if you don't listen. Listening helps you to learn; learning helps you to understand; understanding makes you wise; and being wise helps you . . . to listen even better!

Who knew that a little more time over the green-bean casserole could make you wise? Try it next time!

11

You would think that if people saw somebody put noodles up her nose, they would realize right away just how stupid it is and wouldn't put noodles up their noses. But a lot of noodle-nosers are just doing what they saw some other noodle-noser do.

It's just amazing how often we copy dumb things other people do, for no good reason at all. Most kids who start to cheat on tests, or skateboard down dangerous streets, or play with fireworks, or talk to strangers on the Internet, or start to steal things from stores, or smash people's mailboxes just for fun, or smoke cigarettes, or do drugs, or a hundred other dumb and dangerous things start doing them by copying other kids.

So, the first time your folks see you shoving noodles up your nose or copying something your friends do, they'll most likely hit you with the famous annoying saying, "If your friend jumped off a bridge, would you do it, too?"

This is not a question your parents actually want you to answer. (In fact, there are a whole bunch of annoying questions in this book that you're not supposed to answer, which makes them even *more* annoying than the others. Your parents' fancy name for them would be "rhetorical questions.") Of course you wouldn't jump off a bridge. Your folks know that and you know that. They don't expect you to say no (or yes, because then you look *really* stupid). But if you want to fool them next time, you could respond by saying, "That's a *rhetorical* question, Mom (or Dad)."

It's natural to copy some things other people do. That's how we learn everything we know. We see other people do something and then we do it. That's how we learn to walk, play games, add numbers, and speak clearly. Now, it may seem like there's no difference in copying somebody who's hitting a ball and copying somebody who's putting noodles up his or her nose. Both skills come from copying, but one will help you learn to play baseball and one will just fill your nose with tomato sauce. What your parents are trying to teach you is to learn to copy useful things, not stupid things.

The problem is that copying stupid things that don't matter can lead to copying dangerous things that do matter. You can graduate from noodles in the nose to skateboarding in traffic, from throwing eggs on Halloween to breaking store windows, or from stealing your friend's jelly beans to stealing a stranger's car.

It's not easy at all to learn the difference between useful and stupid things. Jumping off a bridge is a silly example (don't tell your parents) because only a dummy would jump off a bridge just to copy a friend. But what about everything else: what they wear, what they say, the way they treat people and animals — should you copy them or not?

One way to figure it out is to look carefully at the people you're about to copy. Are these people that you admire for a reason other than that they're just "cool" and "popular"? One of the really silly and sad things about the world we live in is that many people are famous for doing nothing! They may be famous just because they're pretty or handsome. They never saved a kid from a burning building. They never fought bravely in a war. They never composed beautiful music or painted a gorgeous picture or wrote a great book or made a movie that taught you good things about life. These famous people are famous just for being famous. They have done nothing! Copying people who have done nothing is stupid.

In your school, too, there are people who are popular and you may want to copy them just because they're popular. You may think that if you copy them, you'll be popular, too. Being popular in school is the little version of being famous for nothing in the big world.

Now, if you're in a great school with great teachers and great students with great values, the most popular kids will be the ones who help other kids the most, let everyone into their group, and always try to be kind and helpful. You probably already know this, but most schools are not like that. Mostly it's just the good-looking kids or the kids who are good at sports who are popular. The thing to remember is to copy people who are worth copying!

Your best test about what to copy and what not to copy is the "I'm just not sure" test. If you're not sure whether to copy something or not, don't copy it. If you're not 100% sure, there's no reason to do it. That worked for me, and maybe it will work for you.

When you learn to think for yourself, you can be yourself; and then when you learn to be yourself, you can know yourself; and when you learn to know yourself, you can really fall in love with somebody else; and when you fall in love with somebody else, you can get married and know that your marriage will last for a long time; and then when you get married, you can have children of your own; and then when you have children of your own, you'll be ready to ask your kid, who has just learned how to put noodles up his nose, "If your friend jumped off a bridge, would you jump, too?"

It's amazing how many really big life lessons begin with noodles.

12

I used to think that it would be neat to let an umpire live in the basement of my house. When I thought my folks were not being fair to me, I thought it would be cool to call my umpire out of the basement and ask him to call my parents out. No luck! The only umpires I ever got were my parents. Mostly they were fair, but there was one thing I never liked. In baseball you get three strikes before you're out, and in my house I got called "out" lots of times with only two strikes.

When my folks told me something I had to do, I usually didn't do it. Then they would say, "I'm not gonna tell you again!" That was strike one, and it told me that the next time I would be out — which meant I would be grounded, busted, or even *so* busted. But this was just two strikes. I would have had a third chance in a baseball game, but unfortunately, my house was not run by the rules of major league baseball.

"I'm not gonna tell you again" is your last warning before being called out. I know it doesn't make sense that baseball seems more fair than my folks (and yours), but that's the way it is. Believe it or not, there's a good reason that parents lay down the law about how many strikes they're willing to take.

You see, you basically have one-and-a-half jobs. Going to school and doing your work for school is your one big job. Then there's your job of mastering your video games or knowing what's hot and what's not. That's half a job. Now, your parents have many jobs. They work to make money to pay for school clothes and video games so that you can do your one-and-a-half jobs. They have to take care of the house you live in and make sure you always have bags of snacks that end in "-itoes." They have to make sure you get taken to doctors and dentists and barbers, and they have to feed you real food once in a while. And they have to do all of those things for themselves, too!

That's a lot of jobs. Sometimes, they need help, and they would like to get your help without having to ask you a zillion more times to put your shoes away when they've already asked you once.

"I'm not gonna tell you again" is like a test to see if you really appreciate what your folks do for you every single day. Doing what they ask you to do as soon as they ask is an important way to show that you love and respect the people who take care of you. Saying you love them is good, too, but believe it or not, it's not as good as *showing* them you love them by doing the things they ask you to do. Your doing makes their doing easier.

Once you leave home, you may think that your "I'm not gonna tell you again" days are over. Actually, your most serious "I'm not gonna tell you again" days are just beginning. In college your professors tell you what to read and when to hand in your work and that's it. They don't tell you again. They don't call you in your dorm room to see if you're doing your homework. They don't remind you in class every day how many days are left before your work is due. They don't even tell you that they're not gonna tell you what they just told you again.

Then, when you get a job, your boss might not even give you *one* "I'm not gonna tell you again" warning. You might just get fired.

I remember days when as a grown-up I wished that

there had been somebody around who'd nag me to re-member to turn out the lights or to do my laundry because I only had one pair of clean underwear left to wear for the rest of the week. But it doesn't exactly work to say to your-self, "I'm not gonna tell you again!"

So when you think about it, you're lucky to get even two strikes when you're growing up. Still, I think having umpires with black uniforms and one guy with a mask and chest protector would be a great idea for every home. Unfortunately, so far, I'm the only one who thinks so.

13

My parents said everything in this book to me at least once when I was growing up, except one: I never got asked "Were you raised in a zoo?" because I actually *was* raised in a zoo. My grandfather Leo (the Lion) Gellman was a zoo-keeper at the Milwaukee Zoo, and I would spend many weekends with him feeding rye bread to the giraffes and mandelbread (which is a kind of cookie) to the monkeys on Monkey Island.

Grandpa taught me to love animals, but he also taught me to understand the difference between animals and people. The big difference isn't that animals have fur and fangs or hides and horns; it's that animals don't know right from wrong and people do — or at least they should. He would explain to me that animals do what they want to do when they want to do it and where they want to do it. They poop where they want and they growl when they want and they fight when they want, and almost nobody can tell them not to. This isn't a bad thing, Grandpa explained to me, it's just an animal thing.

Of course, people are animals, too. We eat and sleep and poop, just like all the other animals. But remembering that we're animals means that we have to eat right, stay clean, and get rest. All animals need good healthy food and clean coats of fur or feathers or scales or skin, too. For humans this means eating more fruits and vegetables and less sugar and doughnuts (which are mostly sugar anyway) and taking a bath or a shower at least once a year. (Don't

tell your parents I said that!) We also need to sleep every night and to remember to brush our fangs (I mean teeth) before we go to bed.

All these things come naturally to other animals (okay, maybe not the toothbrushing), but for some reason they're hard for human animals to learn. We may be the smartest animal, but sometimes we're not that smart when it comes to taking care of ourselves.

We're *more* than just animals, though, because we can control ourselves and we can do the right thing. That's why your parents nag you after you spill your food on your shirt, put a banana in your ear, spit out your juice when you laugh, yell and scream in a restaurant, break things, sit down on the clean couch with your muddy clothes, put your shoes on the coffee table, belch after gulping down some soda pop, or — how can I say this without seeming like I was raised in a zoo? — pass wind.

People have a higher law to obey than animals. You don't have to go to a zoo to know that. The first time you see your dog pee on the rug or your cat shred the sofa, you can see that there are things animals do because they don't know any better. They take what they want unless a stronger animal keeps them away, and they growl, hiss, or bite when they're angry. We don't — or at least we shouldn't.

Instead, we use our words (preferably without word-slime) to try to work things out.

When I was a kid, sometimes I needed to remember to love and respect people as much as I loved the animals at Grandpa's zoo. Once I told Grandpa that I liked the monkeys on Monkey Island better than a boy in my school named Dick who had punched me once. Grandpa told me that maybe the monkeys were better than Dick, but even Dick had to be better than Simon the Gorilla, who threw his poop at Grandpa when he didn't bring him carrots. I told him that it wouldn't surprise me if Dick threw his poop, too. Grandpa Leo laughed and we took out some rye bread and headed to the giraffes.

We both knew that Grandpa was right.

14

Just about the only thing you can control in your life when you're a kid is what you wear, and when your folks try to control even that, you might give up believing that your life will *ever* be yours. That's why most kids get so angry when their parents start telling them what they can and can't wear.

Maybe you've fought some clothes wars in your own house. There are wars over pants worn low enough to show boxers, baseball hats worn sideways, and T-shirts that hang to your knees. However, I think the biggest clothes wars going on today are about belly buttons. A lot of parents just freak about girls' low-rise pants and skirts that show belly buttons — not to mention short shorts and halter tops that show more skin than fabric.

If you have an older brother or sister, you've probably heard the wars over spiky or dyed hair; or body piercings that include rings and studs put through ears, tongues, belly buttons, eyebrows, and places I have not been told about yet. And maybe you've even been on the front lines of wars about tattoos, glow-in-the-dark hair colors, do-rags, platform shoes, shirts without collars, too much makeup, sunglasses at night, and T-shirts with word-slime on them.

If you put on any of these things before you head out the door, you'll probably get turned around and sent back to your room to re-dress, usually with the famous saying: "You can't leave this house looking like that!"

To avoid the parent-forced re-dress (let's just call it the PFR), you have a few moves, none of which are that good. You can climb out your window and try to find a family to live with who likes your look. This move doesn't work too well because of the noise you make (or the legs you break) when you go slamming into the ground from your second-story window, and it's of absolutely no use to kids who live on the upper floors of tall apartment buildings.

Another thing you could try is to come down to breakfast covered up in a big long coat. This idea can sometimes work in the winter, but in warm weather it's just no good. Leaving the house in a buttoned-up coat in the summer makes you look like a spy, which will certainly arouse your parents' suspicion (unless they are spies and you and your brothers and sisters are Spy Kids) and then you're going to get hit with the dreaded PFR — and then you will miss your bus or be late for school.

The most common defense is the argument "Everybody dresses this way." There are two problems with this direct approach. The first is that your parents will say, "I don't care if everybody dresses this way because *you're not everybody*," and they may even point out several examples of other kids who don't wear pants that barely cover their butts. Or else you'll hear the annoying saying we discussed earlier: "If your friends jumped off a bridge, would you do it, too?"

And finally there is the sad move in which you plead with them not to make you re-dress. You end your pitch with, "Do you want me to dress like a dork?" The risk here is that they may hug or kiss you and whisper into your ear, "But honey, you *are* a dork." If they say that, you really *are* out of moves, and you better just submit to the inevitable PFR.

Your best move, though, is to talk to your parents. You'll tell them that what you wear is like a uniform. The jocks all dress a certain way; the burnouts all dress a certain way; the preppy kids all dress a certain way; the Goths all dress a certain way; the chess-club kids all dress a certain way; and you and your cool friends all dress a certain way. You might say that your clothes are like your entrance card into your group and being forced to change your clothes is the same as being forced to change your group.

Unfortunately, your best speech probably won't change anything because your parents have a good speech, too. Their best point is that how you look sometimes affects how you're treated and what people think of you. Dressing like a rebel makes people think you don't respect authority, whether it's true or not. Sexy-looking clothes tell people that you want them to look at your outside first (whether it's true or not), and there's much more to you than that. Clothes speak, and your parents are trying to teach you that.

Besides, any group of friends that needs a uniform doesn't sound like a whole lot of fun, anyway. Uniforms worn to keep other kids in school out of your group just keep you surrounded by people who are exactly like you. If you want to grow up, you need to meet, learn from, and understand people who are not exactly like you. If your clothes keep you from doing that, well then, it's time to get new clothes.

15

In the 1939 movie *The Wizard of Oz,* Dorothy (played by the actress Judy Garland) sings a great song called "Somewhere Over the Rainbow." I especially love the question at the end of the song: "If happy little bluebirds fly beyond the rainbow, why oh why can't I?"

In my house, and maybe in yours, the answer was simple: "Your mom or dad grounded the bluebirds!"

One of the really bad things about being a kid is that you never get a lawyer. If you're an adult on trial, you get to hire a lawyer who can defend you (and even if you have no money, the court has to pay for a lawyer to defend you). But when you're a kid and your parents accuse you of doing something bad — or doing something good, but too late, or doing nothing when you should have been doing something, or just standing near some other person at some party who did something bad that you should have stopped — you don't get a lawyer; you don't get to decide if you want a judge or a jury; you don't get to call witnesses; and you don't get a trial. What you get is grounded.

Grounded is the absolutely best word to describe having all your freedoms taken away because your parents are mad at you for something you did or didn't do. When you're not grounded, you can fly through life like a bird or a plane or Superman, but when you're grounded you're not allowed to fly *anywhere*.

Being grounded is like being given a time-out when you are younger. Little kids get a time-out. Bigger kids get

grounded. Also, a time-out is MUCH shorter than being grounded. A time-out usually lasts a few minutes, but being grounded can last a few days, or, if you are SO GROUNDED, maybe even a few weeks, or even months. (In all my studies of these things, I never heard of any kid being grounded for more than a year though.)

There are many levels of grounding, of course, and your sentence depends on what you did or didn't do and how your parents are feeling about what you did or didn't do. There's light grounding, where you come home from school and can't go out anywhere, but you can still use the phone and the computer to IM your friends. Then there's the heavy fully loaded grounding where you can't go out, use the phone, watch TV, listen to music, or use the computer. (The record for a kid enduring heavy fully loaded grounding without going crazy is three weeks and one day.)

The first lesson of being grounded is pretty obvious: your parents are in charge. You don't make the rules; they do. You don't decide what you want to do; they do. It's not too different from the way you train a dog not to poop in the house. The dog has to learn that you're its master and not the other way around.

Now, this isn't a lesson that any kid wants to hear, particularly since it means being compared to a dog. But there is good news! The second lesson is a much greater lesson that will last your whole life and help you to be a good and happy person.

The second lesson is that actions have consequences. What you do now determines what happens to you in the future. The Hindus call this *karma*, and parents call it grounding, but it's kind of the same idea: everything you do matters. Even little things like petting your dog or kissing your parents good night or saying "please" and "thank you" cause other good things to happen in your life.

You can imagine how a little rock falling high on a snowy mountain might cause a huge avalanche. Well, karma and being grounded are sort of like that. A little good thing you do can cause an avalanche of good to happen in your life. And on the other side, a little bad thing you do (like kicking the dog or yelling at your parents or never saying please or thank you) can start an avalanche of bad things. It's usually not good or bad luck; it's the good or bad deeds that you do. Even when it looks like you can get away with bad stuff — or that nobody notices the good stuff you do — karma is still working, and someday you'll see the results.

You can be angry with your parents for grounding you, but you might also want to think about what you did that made them ground you. If you think that your parents were too strict with you, go talk to them about it. You can learn what really matters to them, and they can learn what kind of warnings you need. You can tell them that you need to practice being a grown-up so that you can learn how to be a grown-up, and they can explain why they feel that some of the risks you take are just not worth it.

It's worth being grounded to have that kind of conversation with your parents. You just want to be free and happy and fly over the rainbow. They just don't want you to crash.

You're both right.

16

You can stare at a beautiful sunset or a majestic mountain or singing birds in the tree outside your bedroom window, but staring at people just isn't the same kind of thing.

If you just got hit by a hundred cream pies, you could understand why people would be staring at you. If you went to school naked, you could understand why people would be staring at you. If you jumped into the shark tank at the aquarium, you could understand why people would be staring at you. But if you're just walking down the street, sitting in a chair, or eating an ice-cream cone, there is no reason for anybody to stare at you.

But you and I both know that sometimes it's hard not to stare. When somebody is eight feet tall or really, really fat or really, really beautiful or disabled in some way that seems impossible to ignore, it's hard not to stare. If you stare at somebody like that in your class or stare at the people sitting next to you in a restaurant, your parents will probably tell you in a hushed and urgent whisper, "Don't stare!" (And then they might kick you under the table.)

Staring makes people feel uncomfortable. Just ask somebody who looks really different. Ask somebody who has to use a wheelchair how it feels to be stared at. Ask somebody who has been burned and whose face is covered with scars how it feels to be stared at. Ask somebody with no arms or legs how it feels to be stared at. They'll probably tell you that being stared at hurts their feelings. It

makes them feel like they don't fit in and shouldn't be with other people.

You must have had a day when people stared at you so much that you felt like crawling inside your desk. Maybe you rushed out of the house and dressed in an orange shirt and green pants. Or maybe you had a booger hanging out of your nose and nobody told you. Or maybe a pigeon pooped on your head. You felt goofy enough to begin with, but the whole thing became ten times worse because people were staring at you all day long. So, why would you want to put other people through that?

What makes staring at people wrong is not just that it's rude; it's that it makes us think about how we're all different instead of how we're all the same. Even though people have different shapes and personalities and talents, we're all basically the same. We all want to be happy; we all need friends; we all need to be loved; and we all want to do what we're good at. Thinking about how we're all the same pulls us together. It reminds us that everyone we meet is more like a friend than a stranger.

Hey, we all have a different skin color and wear different shoe sizes, but we all have the same color blood inside us. Learning to look beyond appearances helps you feel better about being a person here on planet Earth — and of course, it also helps you not to stare.

Here's one last thing to think about. Even though the people you're staring at may look strange to you, to other people like them, you're probably the one who looks strange. I learned this one day when I was at the Special Olympics, a sports competition for kids with disabilities. When I left the stadium, I was suddenly surrounded by about a hundred kids on wheelchairs who were going to compete in wheelchair basketball. I was the only person walking, and they were wheeling themselves way faster than I could walk. Then one of the kids smiled at me and told the others, "Hey, slow down, don't run him over. He can't go as fast as us." The kid smiled at me, and I smiled right back.

That day, I learned that it's okay to stare — if everyone's smiling.

17

I don't care if everybody has one. . . . I'm not buying it for you!

The main reason you have clothes is that your school has rules against coming to school naked! So you need to get some clothes. You need to buy warm clothes to wear in cold weather, otherwise your fingers might freeze and fall off (and you need your fingers to play video games). You also need to buy books to read, because books make your mind healthy, flexible, creative, and strong.

So, while there are lots of things you truly need to buy, there are also lots of things you don't need at all. You don't need a helicopter. You don't need a spaceship. You don't need poisonous snakes. You don't need those pocket-knives with a hundred different blades. Even if you want these things, you don't need them. Yes, the list of things you don't need is HUGE.

If you can't figure out the difference between things you just want and the things you really need, your folks will probably help you out by saying, "I don't care if everybody has one. . . . I'm not buying it for you!"

You learned this when you were old enough to realize that just because you want something doesn't mean that you can get it from your parents. (Grandparents are a different story. Most grandparents love buying things for their grandchildren. I got most of the candy I was allowed to eat from my grandma.) Sometimes your parents won't buy you something you want because it's too expensive and they don't have the money to buy it. It's embarrassing for parents to tell their children that they don't have enough money to pay the rent or mortgage, buy food, *and* get them everything they want. Arguing with your folks can make it even more embarrassing for them.

Even if your folks have the money, they might think that the thing you want is just too expensive for a kid — or anyone, for that matter — to have. Some parents think that buying a handbag that costs a ridiculous amount of money, just to store empty candy wrappers, crumpled notes that you passed in class, a few cheap pens and dull pencils, your plastic hairbrush full of split ends or dandruff, a container of lip gloss, and a half-eaten bag of chips is crazy. Then, the several-hundred-dollar purse just gets crammed into a stinky locker during gym class.

I knew a girl who really wanted a Kate Spade handbag like the ones she saw other girls carrying around, and there was no way her mom was going to buy such an expensive bag for her. So, she asked her mom if she could babysit for her little brother and do other chores around the house for money. Her mom agreed, and she worked for many months, saved up the money, and bought the bag with her own money. When I asked her to show me the bag, she said she kept it at home. I was surprised and asked her why. She said, "Are you kidding? That bag is way too expensive

to take out of the house. I would be afraid that somebody would steal it from me, or that I might spill soup on it at lunch." Go figure.

But she did have a point: expensive things like iPods and dirt bikes can be magnets for people who steal things. If you lose something cheap it's a bummer, but if you lose something expensive it's a serious bummer.

Do you even know for sure that you *really* want everything you ask for? Sometimes advertising on television makes us want things we don't really need. I used to want all the toys I saw advertised on the Saturday morning cartoon shows (now they have Cartoon Network on cable TV, where you can watch cartoons 24 hours a day). But I didn't really want that stuff; I just thought I wanted it because it looked so good to me on TV. Back then, ads included lots of stuff that you never actually got when you bought the toy. Ads for miniature army tanks, battleships, and fighter planes had fire and smoke coming from the guns, but when I got the models, there was no fire and no smoke — they weren't even painted! I learned then that the things people say to make you want to buy something don't always have much to do with the real world.

When your parents say, "I don't care if everyone else has one. . . . I'm not buying it for you," they're asking you to slow down and think about the influence that other things and other people are trying to have on your life. Ads may tell you about new and cool and great stuff that will make your life easier or more fun, but when you're a kid, it's still your parents' job to figure out if what the ads are trying to sell you is good for you.

The real reason your parents don't buy you what you want all the time is to teach you to be an individual. There's a lot of pressure in your life to be the same as other kids your age. Some of that pressure comes from other kids; some comes from advertising; and some of it comes from inside of you when you feel that you just want to fit in. But the best things about you are the things that only you have, like your talents and your personality. These are the things that make you who you are and show other people how special you are.

It's just as much fun — no, it's *more* fun — to have something that nobody else has instead of what everybody else already has. After all, sometimes new styles start with people who have the guts to dress a little differently or to think that some stuff that nobody thought was cool before is actually pretty cool. You, too, could be a style setter when you try to be like you instead of trying to be like them.

18

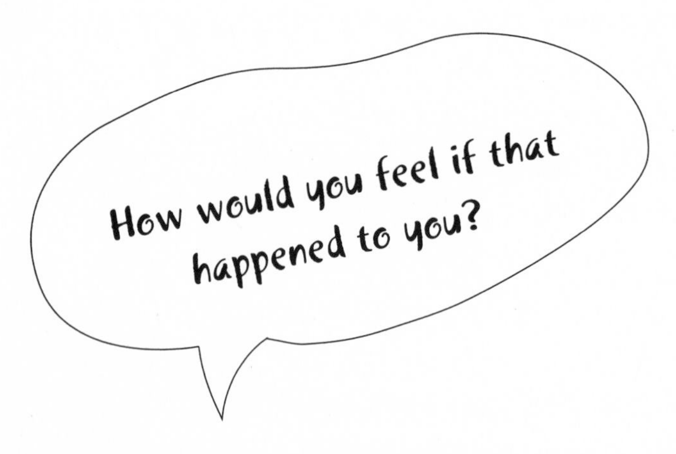

One of my favorite cartoon characters was Wile E. Coyote. He was a cartoon coyote who was always trying to catch and eat Road Runner — a superfast bird who mostly ran around saying, "Meep! Meep!" In every cartoon, Wile E. Coyote would get blown up or fall off a cliff or have a giant boulder fall on his head. He never got killed because nobody ever gets killed in a cartoon, but he sure did get burned and bashed and shmooshed a lot.

Each time Wile E. got wiped out, I thought it was the funniest thing I'd ever seen. But now I wonder whether there was some part of those cartoons that taught me a bad thing: to laugh at other people when something embarrassing or bad happens to them.

Sometimes it's hard to figure out when it's okay to laugh and when it's not. It's okay to laugh at your friend if he or she gets hit by a cream pie. I also think it's okay to laugh at your friend if he or she gets hit by a fruit pie. In general, pies are not dangerous (unless you eat a whole pie in half an hour, in which case you might get very sick). But I don't think it's okay to laugh at your friend if he or she gets hit by a cookie, because cookies are hard and they could scratch an eye. (I'm not sure how I feel about muffins.)

The thing is, getting hit by a pie is funny, even if your friend feels a little embarrassed by the pie attack. It's good not to take stuff too seriously, and laughing off a pie attack seems to me to be the right thing to do. But if your friend is being teased or even if somebody who isn't your friend is being teased, insulted, tripped, hit, or hurt, it's up to you to stand up for that person and try to stop it. Why? Because of the annoying but important parental saying, "How would you feel if that happened to you?"

Being able to imagine just how it would feel to experience something is called *compassion*, which we have talked about before. If you're going to be a compassionate person, you'll want to try to stop all the things that make other kids feel like dirt. And believe me, there are a lot of them:

When someone is always the last one picked for a team

in gym class because he isn't good at a sport, it can make life terrible for that kid. If you're a compassionate person, someday you might think about picking the worst player on your team first. That would make the kid's day.

Some kids are teased because they don't wear the latest cool clothes. But if you're a compassionate person, you know that what matters about people isn't what they wear on the outside, but what they're like on the inside. So you'll tell them that they look good even if they don't look cool.

Some kids get teased for being slow learners. If you're a compassionate person, and there's a kid in your class who's having trouble, you'll offer to help him study for class.

If you're going to be a compassionate person, you'll feel the pain of klutzes, dorks, "losers," slow kids, and the big kids who get called "fat pigs." And if you're going to be a compassionate person, you'll never even use the words "klutz," "dork," "loser," or "fat pig" — because you'll know that being called an ugly name is the worst feeling in the world.

If you were in a bad place, wouldn't you want people to come over to try to cheer you up? If you see a kid whose pet just died, you could go over and tell her that you're sorry about what happened. If you see a kid sitting alone, maybe you could ask that kid to sit with you and your friends. Lunchtime at school is a really good time to practice compassion.

Compassion really is all about feeling what other people are feeling. Once you do that, it changes your life and it changes other kids' lives. Compassion keeps you from being selfish and gets you out of the habit of just thinking about yourself and makes you want a life of kindness and good deeds. When you're able to feel the pain of others, you'll be amazed at the things you'll want to do with your life, other than just playing sports and video games, listening to music and going shopping.

"How would you feel if that happened to you?" is the question that gets many compassionate people to volunteer their time in a soup kitchen serving food to poor, hungry people. When you can feel the pain of people who need your help, then you can start to help change the world.

One great person who helped poor people was a Catholic nun in India named Mother Teresa. She once said, "We are not called to do great things. We are called to do little things with great love." You can do little things with great love, and you can change the world. I know it's hard to believe that all this begins by not laughing at the kid who spilled his hot soup on his pants or asking a kid with no friends to have lunch with you and your friends, but that's how compassion grows. It starts with soup and it ends with the world.

Compassion is one of the biggest and best lessons your parents will ever teach you, but it may be one of the hardest things to learn. So there's no better time to start than today. There's not a moment to waste. I'm serious. Wile E. Coyote is right behind you!

Meep! Meep!

19

You can never really know if the person you just met is nice or not nice. Sometimes people act nice, but they're really mean deep down and are hiding their meanness. You need a niceness test, and I have one for you. If people are mean to animals, they're going to be mean to people, and you should stay away from them. I guess *some* people could be mean to animals and nice to people, but I've never met someone like that. My test usually works.

Some kids think it's cool or funny to pull a cat's tail, or poke their fingers into a dog's eyes, or throw rocks at squirrels, or do other mean things to animals that they don't think are cruel but really are.

If your parents see you pull the cat's tail just to see it

jump five feet in the air and yowl, they'll probably say to you in a stern voice, "Don't pull the cat's tail!" Or they may ask you a version of the question from the last chapter, "How would you feel if somebody pulled your tail?" which, I admit, is a stupid question since you don't have a tail. (Or do you?)

When people hurt their pets by hitting them or starving them, those animals may run away or turn mean. If the pets are lucky, they'll be found and taken to animal shelters and someday adopted by a loving family that will never hurt them again. You might want to find out how you can support the no-kill shelters in your community because they help a lot of cats who have had their tails pulled (and a lot of other animals, too).

Near my home, there is a great shelter that also has two big buses filled with cages for cats and dogs. On the side of one of the buses is a cartoon by Patrick McDonnell, a cartoonist who loves animals. It shows a cat thinking: "I know what it's like to be alone in a cage . . . waiting for a kindness from a stranger. You wait . . . and wait . . . hoping . . . praying . . . thinking, 'Life shouldn't be like this.' You know you can do more . . . Be more . . . You hold onto the dream . . . You just wish someday you could share it with someone." The shelter sends the buses all over the country so that people who may not even know where to find their local animal shelter can see animals available for adoption and can give them loving homes.

We should treat animals just as if they were furry little people (except of course for lizards and snakes, who we should treat as if they were scaly little people), and we should treat people as if they were non-furry animals. Nothing alive should have its tail pulled or its feelings hurt. The only exception I can think of is when you walk into a dark room and accidentally step on your cat's tail. (Chances are your cat won't be too happy though — accident or not.)

The big reason to be kind to animals isn't just that it's good for the animals, but that it's good for you. You see, when you become mean, it's like dripping red paint on a

white shirt. Sometimes you can get the stain out, but sometimes the stain stays in the shirt and ruins it. Cruelty is a stain on the best part of you. It's hard to get it out of your life once you let it in.

Cruelty isn't something you catch like a cold. Nobody is really nice one day and then wakes up really mean the next day and forever after. The way people get bad or good is in little steps, day by day, until one day they're really nice or really mean.

Kids who pick on weak animals learn to pick on weaker kids. So, leave the cat's tail alone — then stand back and wait for all the niceness to flood into your life. Your parents — and your cat — will thank you for it.

20

Did what I just said go in one ear and out the other?

If your doctor took a picture of your brain and showed it to your parents, there are some days when your parents just wouldn't believe what they'd see. The picture would show that inside your skull there is a squishy gray glob of goo called a brain. On these days your parents would say to your doctor, "Look, we want to thank you for taking a picture of Sammy's brain, but we don't believe that it's really there. Just today we told Sammy to do something five times and it didn't get done. Now, if Sammy really did have a brain in between his ears, what we said would not have gone in one ear and right out the other."

I know that it's hard to listen to everything your parents, teachers, coaches, grandparents, sitters, tutors, bus drivers, hall monitors, gym teachers, uncles, aunts, and crossing guards tell you to do. There are just so many people telling you what to do that you can hardly keep track of them — never mind what they're actually telling you to do! But it's safe to say that this is one thing that is not about to change here on planet Earth as long as you're a kid. That's the bad news. The good news is that every one of those people wants to help you! Let me explain.

One rule of being a kid is that you're supposed to listen to almost everybody, and do at least the important things they tell you to do right away. But your parents are supposed to help you decide what the important things are. "Did what I just told you go in one ear and out the other?"

is a way for your parents to tell you that you missed an important thing.

Listening is the hardest skill you can learn. Surfing is easier than listening. Wrestling alligators is easier than listening. Changing the top lightbulb at the top of the Empire State Building is easier than listening. But once you've actually *heard* something, it's hard to know if what you're being told is important or if it's just one of the million things you hear that doesn't really matter at all. If you're not sure which is which, you should just ask if this is a "do it right now" order or a "do it when you can" order. Your parents will probably laugh and then tell you which it is.

Take a guess: how many times do you think your parents usually have to tell you something before you'll finally do it? Now, go to your folks and ask them how many times *they* think they have to ask you before you do what they've asked. I bet your number is lower than their number.

It's just not enough to listen — it's important to act. That's the only way to prove to your parents that your skull is filled with more than air and gray goo — besides getting the doctor to take a picture of your skull that shows all of the love and respect you have for the people who care about you floating around inside your head. Unfortunately, I don't think the brain scan machines are quite that good, yet.

21

Use your head for more than just a hat rack!

The most important muscle in your whole body is your brain. Like all your muscles, if you don't exercise it, it gets weak. If you do exercise it, it gets stronger and stronger.

Brains need exercise to stay strong. You know some brain exercises and so do I. Crossword puzzles, chess, math problems, and riddles are all famous brain exercises. There are other brain exercises that are just as good and don't require that you know the three-letter word for "a long-haired ox of the Tibetan highlands" (yak). These are the exercises your parents want you to do when they say, "Use your head for more than just a hat rack!" (I know this may be one of those old-fashioned sayings because not too many people wear hats nowadays, unless they are cowboys or baseball players or wizards or witches.) But in Parent, the saying means that you should think for yourself before you do something stupid all over again.

Grown-ups are not exactly calling you stupid when they say, "Use your head for more than just a hat rack!" They're really just saying that you're being lazy-brained. Being lazy-brained is different from being stupid. Lazy-brained people are smart, but they just forget to think about what they're doing sometimes. What grown-ups are saying in the language of Parent is that they want you to use your head (and the brain inside your head) to *think*.

Of course, you're thinking all the time. You're thinking about how long it is until lunch, what music to listen to, who said what about whom, how short you can wear your skirt without getting told "You can't leave this house looking like that," who to IM first when you get home, and how close you are to being able to eat anything made of chocolate. But using your head for more than a hat rack means using your brain to figure out small things so that one day your brain will be strong enough to figure out big things, too.

All of your daily comforts — from your toilet to your toaster, from your VCR to your video games, from your can opener to your car — everything we use was created by people who used their head for more than a hat rack. Now it's your turn to exercise your brain and figure out what "more" YOUR head can do.

Once people thought that the world was flat, but then smart people used their heads for more than a hat rack and proved that the world was round (or sort of round). Once people thought that when you had a cough or a cold you should have a worm called a leech put on your chest to suck out some of your blood. Then, doctors figured out that when you have a cold and just stay in bed for a while, watch television, and eat chocolate-chip cookies with milk, the cold will go away on its own. You can leave the leeches in the garden.

Our world is better today because years ago lots of smart people used their heads as more than a hat rack. But we still need smart people to find a cure for cancer and all sorts of other diseases that have not been cured yet. Our world needs strong-brained people to figure out how to make fuel for all of our electricity and engines without polluting the air, and to make food without chemicals that might make us sick.

Most of all, our world needs strong-brained people to finally figure out why one sock always seems to escape from the dryer and run away so we can never find it again.

We need to figure out how to make lines in the girls' bathroom shorter and how to make great burgers that don't make you fat. There are still so many mysteries in life that need to be figured out, and the world needs you and your brain to be in top shape to help.

So get going, get thinking, and keep your brain active and strong. And when your parents nag you about a lazy brain, remember that they're not insulting you. They're just telling you that the world is waiting for you and your brain to make a difference.

22

Running is a good thing. It makes you feel good and it gets you to where you're going faster than walking (but not as fast as having your mom or dad drive you). Using scissors is also a good thing. Scissors help you cut pictures of your favorite superstar out of a newspaper or magazine in a neat way so that you don't make your parents angry because you accidentally ripped through a coupon for Pizza Hut. But running with scissors isn't a good thing because if you fall, there's no telling how many limbs you might actually lose.

When your folks say, "Don't run with scissors!" they're not trying to scare you. They're trying to make you realize that you must respect dangerous things, and scissors can be dangerous. Of course, I don't mean those doofy scissors they gave you in kindergarten — you know, the ones with the plastic handles and the dull rounded points that could hardly cut paper. Those scissors could not hurt you unless you stuck them up your nose (and if you did that, you have a different problem — you're a doofus who needs help).

Not everything you use is dangerous and you shouldn't go through your life being afraid of everything you touch. Backpacks are not dangerous (well, okay, they could hurt your back if you load them up). Cell phones are not dangerous (well, okay, some people think they could zap your brain with microwaves). iPods are not dangerous (well, okay, they could blast your eardrums if you play them too loudly). Okay, so everything *can* be a little dangerous in some way — except those yellow plastic ducks you played with in the bathtub when you were a baby.

Every year some kids hurt themselves setting off fireworks, wiping out on those mini four-wheel-drive motorcycles, or shooting loaded guns, and all of them knew that they were running with scissors. And they got hurt anyway.

"Don't run with scissors!" is your first warning that

the things we use in our life can be very helpful or very dangerous, and it's up to you to decide to use them safely. A computer can take you around the world to discover wonderful things about people and places you never knew, or it can bring you to a chat room where some creepy grown-up pretending to be a kid might be trying to meet you. There are lots of scissors in this world, but there's only one you, and your parents won't always be around to warn you. Just remember, if it isn't a yellow plastic duck, watch out!

Respecting the dangerous things we use in our lives is a lesson we learn as a child, but we actually need to use it even more after we become adults. So, if you see your dad

or mom driving too fast, talking on their cell phone while they're driving, or putting too much lighter fluid on the barbecue, it's okay to tell them, "Don't run with scissors!" After all, if they have the right to tell you annoying things that are good for you, every now and then you have the right to tell them annoying things that are good for them!

23

Your parents may call you a drama queen (or king) because you're always making a big deal out of a little deal — like when you cried your eyes out after falling down and getting just a little scrape on your knee, or when you freaked out in the doctor's office when you were about to get a shot, or when you screamed like a prisoner when your parents wouldn't take you where you wanted to go right then and there.

On the other side, there may have been moments when the drama king or drama queen in your house wasn't you, it was your mom or dad. The truth is that sometimes your parents can be the real drama queens (or kings). I remember having many pillow fights with my younger sisters

(Judi and Joanne) and my brother (Larry). Most of those really fun fights were broken up by my mom, who came upstairs to our bedrooms screaming for us to stop the pillow fight right away because (and yes, this is really what she said), "It's all fun and games until somebody loses an eye!"

When she said it for the first time, we all just stood there on the bed for a moment trying to understand what she was talking about. We were wondering how it was possible to get hurt at all in a pillow fight with pillows that didn't even have zippers (not that pillows with zippers are really that dangerous either). Then, we all just fell down laughing. For whatever reason, my mom thought that our pillow fight *could* become a disaster, and we thought that she was just nuts.

Years later, my daughter Mara accused me of saying the very same ridiculous thing to her that my mom had once said to me. She fell down laughing, too. That was the day I realized that maybe, just maybe, my mom was onto something more important than pillow fights.

I always thought that the main job of being a kid was figuring out what's fun. The main job of parents is to figure out what's dangerous. Both jobs are important. But most kids get hurt doing things they think are fun because they don't think about how what they're doing can also be dangerous. Diving into a swimming pool or a lake or the ocean is fun, but if you don't know how deep the water is, you could hit your head and break your neck. Riding your bike is fun, but if you don't look both ways when you cross a street or wear a helmet, you could get hit or fall and crack your head.

Knowing that fun can go with danger is one of the reasons your parents may tell you things that sound silly like, "It's all fun and games until someone loses an eye." It's not that they don't want you to have fun. It's that they want you to be careful when you're having fun and to think about the risks you're taking.

Kids who grow up safe, smart, and fun-loving are the kids who have learned how to manage the risks they take in their lives. Figuring out how risky something is — or how dangerous it has the potential to be — can be one of the most important things you learn to figure out in your life. Smart people can get hurt, lose money, and lose friends all because they didn't learn how to figure out what was risky and what was safe.

When you get older, risks take on new meanings. Kids who drink beer for fun at parties are not only breaking the law, they're also putting themselves in danger. When the parties become violent or when people drink and drive, they can lose way more than an eye; they can lose their lives. The same is true about drugs. Drugs might create the feeling that everything in the whole world is just perfect for now, but those same drugs can fry your brain and ruin your life.

The good news is that if you can just learn to understand risks, your life will be one big happy pillow fight with no sharp zippers anywhere. And nobody will lose an eye.

24

"Practice makes perfect" is just plain wrong! Parents, teachers, and coaches tell you this when you should be practicing something but aren't. They tell you this when you're trying to solve a math problem and you can't or when you're trying to learn how to say, "Could you please tell me where the bus stops?" in Chinese but what you're really saying is, "Could you please stick this egg roll in my ear?" Whenever you mess up something you're trying to learn, some adult will probably throw out the old "practice makes perfect" line.

Grown-ups think they're encouraging you to do better. They think that telling you that practice makes perfect will make you do better, be better, think better, and brush your teeth better. Maybe. But it won't make you perfect.

I used to love watching Michael Jordan play basketball. I think he was just about perfect, but no matter how much I practice basketball, I will never be perfect. The truth is that no matter how much I practice, I won't even be very good. I'm a bad basketball player, and I will be a bad basketball player even if I never sleep or eat and only practice basketball until I fall down and throw up. Practicing basketball can make me a *better* basketball player, but it won't make me a perfect basketball player — like Mike.

So the saying should be, "Practice might not make you perfect, but it will make you better." But you know what? Even "Practice will make you better" isn't always true. If you practice without a good teacher or coach showing you how to do something the right way, you're probably going to be repeating your old mistakes over and over again. So, maybe the saying should be, "Practice makes you better if you're practicing under the guidance of a good teacher or coach."

But even that isn't always true. If you're practicing something that just doesn't fit with how your mind or your body is made, then all the practice in the world, even with good teachers and coaches, isn't going to make *that* much of a difference. If you're a klutz and have bad hand-eye coordination, juggling is probably not going to work for you.

So, then, maybe the saying should be something like this, "Practice makes you better if you have a good teacher or coach and if what you're trying to do is appropriate for the way you're built and the skills you have." But this is way too long and depressing, and it misses the whole point of practicing, which is very simple and very good. What I think the saying should be is "practice makes you the best you can be."

Being perfect is impossible. Even things can't be perfect. There is no perfect circle or perfect machine, and people

are way more complicated than things. Perfect is impossible, but being the best you can be isn't. To get there you need to practice, get good advice, do what you love, and learn to figure out what gifts you've been given to share with the world.

So, the next time some adult tells you that practice makes perfect, you may tell them politely that it might not. That's my advice. I have nothing else to say. I have to go practice my Chinese now. There's an egg roll in my ear.

25

If you have a big butt, I don't mean to insult you, but this is a fact: we have become a big-butted country. Every doctor will tell you that obesity — that is, the kind of extra weight that is so severe it could make you sick — is a big problem in the United States. It's a problem that is just as serious as cancer or some other disease. That's one reason that when your folks see you lying around the house like a couch potato, they might holler, "Get off your rear end!"

When I was a kid, there was no color TV, computers, cell phones, video anything, or MP3 players. We had board games to play when it was raining, but usually, if you wanted to have fun you had to go outside and play ball or ride your bike or play hide-and-seek. I didn't understand it at the time, but all those things I did to have fun made me exercise and kept me healthy.

Today you only need to move one or two fingers to have fun. You can play video games, IM your friends, surf the Internet on a computer, watch a zillion channels on TV, and talk to your friends and snap photos with your own cell phone, all at the same time. You can drink a hundred different sodas and eat a thousand different snacks that end in "-itoes" or "-licious." But all these changes in the way we live can have big bad side effects: they can make us sick, or fat, or both.

When your folks tell you to get off your rear end, they're not saying it just to get you to do something right away. It may sound like they're calling you lazy, but what they're really saying is that they want to make you move around and exercise your body so that you stay healthy.

The only way to fight the butt-busting changes in our lives is to make butt-shrinking decisions. We need to walk, run, jump, swim, hike, bike, and skateboard around the neighborhood and around school. Find a fun hobby that keeps you moving for half an hour a day, at least three or four times a week and you, and your butt, will be just fine.

This isn't just a kid problem — no way. This is also a problem for us adults. I used to be thin, but now I'm too fat. I sit around typing at my computer and riding in cars, and I eat too much. If your mom and dad are overweight, the next time they tell you to get off your rear end, you might want to invite them to take a walk around the block with you. That walk will do two great things: it will give you some time to be with your folks and it will give all of you a chance to be active. Taking family walks is good for your family (and good for your family's butts).

The other meaning of "Get off your rear end" has nothing to do with the size of your butt, but has a lot to do with the size of your dreams. We all have dreams about who we'd like to be in this life. These dreams — well, at least most of them — could come true if we worked hard to

make them real. Working hard means getting off our rear ends and doing something to make our dreams real.

I had a friend who wanted to be a veterinarian and take care of animals. He didn't just wait to finish grade school and then finish high school and then finish college and then finish veterinary school. He rode his bike to the vet's office and he volunteered to help clean out the cages and pet the animals who were scared and straighten up the magazines in the front waiting room. He worked in the vet's office all through high school, and when it came time for him to apply to veterinary school after college, the vet in the office where he cleaned the cages wrote the best letter you ever read telling the school how this young man would make a terrific veterinarian. That letter helped to get him accepted to the school, and now he is a wonderful vet. His dream became real because he got off his rear end and did something about it.

I know one of the guys who discovered the way DNA is put together. (DNA is the stuff that makes our genes, and our genes are like maps inside our body that make us who we are.) His name is Dr. James Watson and he told me that from the time he was fifteen years old, he decided that chemistry was the most important science in the world. From that day on, he got off his rear end and started to read everything he could about chemistry (okay, he was still on his rear end when he was reading, but you know what I mean). Pretty soon he knew more about the chemistry of the human body than any person anywhere.

Then, one day, he and a man named Francis Crick discovered the structure of DNA, and their discovery changed the world. For the first time, we could understand how the body works and what makes us sick. Their discovery was a big deal in healing people from diseases, and it all started when James Watson got off his rear end and began preparing for his dream. When I asked Dr. Watson where he got the push to do all that studying about chemistry, he told me, "My parents just told me to get off my rear end and learn something — so I did."

So, if you want to follow your dreams and maybe even change the world, get to it. The beginning of all your dreams starts in the space you make between your butt and the couch.

26

This saying sounds like it was first said to comfort somebody who had been bucked off a horse. The idea seems to be that after a horse throws you, the best thing to do is to get off the ground, shake off the dust, and get back up on the horse. I don't ride horses much, but people who do tell me that this is very good falling-off-a-horse advice — unless you break something when you fall, in which case you should pick yourself up, dust yourself off, and go to the hospital right away.

The meaning of "Pick yourself up, dust yourself off, and start all over again" is a little different when you're not on a horse. Your folks will probably say this after you fail at something and don't want to try it again because you're afraid of failing again. So, then they tell you not to give up, and to keep trying until you get good at what you're lousy at doing right now. What they're trying to tell you is that the only way to get better at something is to fail at doing it and to try again and again.

At first, the meaning of this saying in Parent may seem to be the same as "Practice makes perfect." Actually, it's quite different. "Practice makes perfect" is about how to get better. "Pick yourself up . . ." is about how to deal with what happens when you're not getting better and you fall down.

"Pick yourself up, dust yourself off, and start all over again," is really about how we deal with failure. There are three things this saying is really telling us that will help us deal with messing up and getting back on the horse of life. (The horse of life? I know that sounds silly, but it's just one of those things that writers think sound deep.)

The first step is to "pick yourself up," because you have to believe in yourself before you can recover from your mistakes. Everybody makes mistakes. Every person fails, and the bigger the thing is that you're trying to do, the more chances you have to fail. Just remember that you are a terrific person who was meant to succeed, not meant to fail.

Nobody has ever been born who was just like you or could do the special things you can do. So, you need to be proud of yourself if you expect other people to respect you, and you need to believe in your ability to stand right up and try again.

The second step to changing your life for the better is to "dust yourself off." Dusting yourself off means learning to forget about the past and to concentrate on the present and the future. I live in New York, and when people here say "Forget about it," sometimes it comes out sounding like "fuhgehdaboudit" because of their New York accents. So that's the second secret of life: *fuhgehdaboudit!*

Forgetting about failure is hard, but if you don't move on you will be stuck thinking about what you did wrong rather than what you can do right. So just *fuhgehdaboudit!*

After you've realized that you're not a failure, and after you *fuhgehdaboudit*, then it's time to "start all over again." Trying again is really more important than succeeding because most people don't succeed at any hard thing they do for the first time. What separates the winners from the losers is that the winners are willing to fail over and over again, and the losers quit after they fail once or twice.

Nobody can force you to try except you. The poet T.S.

Eliot once wrote, "For us, there is only the trying. The rest is not our business." He meant that if you pay attention to trying, the winning will take care of itself.

As you grow up, life is going to kiss you and life is going to bump you around. When life kisses you, just remember to be grateful and share the kisses you get with people who have not been kissed enough. And when life bumps you — look for the horse!

27

Just who do you think you are?

Sometimes silly questions turn out to be really important questions, and sometimes silly questions are just . . . silly questions. "How much wood could a woodchuck chuck if a woodchuck could chuck wood?" is a silly question — and even after you think about it, it's still silly. The question "Just who do you think you are?" sounds silly, too — you think you're you, and, in fact, you *are* you — but this is the kind of silly question that's actually really deep and big. But you might miss that because, of course, it is a question written in Parent. This is not a question about who you think you are. This is a question about whether or not you have humility.

If you look it up in a dictionary, *humility* is a word that means you're humble. If you're humble, it means you have humility. This is why I hate dictionaries. They sometimes tell you what a word means by using another word you don't understand to define the word you didn't understand in the first place.

Humility really means that you never think that you're better than other people. If you're humble, you never think of telling someone to get you something if you can get it for yourself. If you're humble, you never talk about how much money your parents have even if they have a lot of it. If you're humble, you never talk about your grades even if they're terrific. The opposite of humble is *arrogant*, and it's a word I hope will never be used to describe you.

If you read history, you'll discover how many of the

really great people in the world were humble. Abe Lincoln came from poor farming parents and remained humble even after he became president. Mahatma Gandhi led India to freedom, but he was so humble that when he died he was totally poor. And the best praise of Moses is that he was a very humble man. Being great and being humble go together.

I know a great golfer who became a golf announcer. His name is Ken Venturi. When he won his first big golf tournament he was very proud of himself, and when he told his dad, his dad was proud of him, too. But after he went on and on telling his dad how great he was, his dad said to him in a quiet but firm voice, "Son, when you're good you can tell other people, but when you're great other people will tell you." Arrogance is when you tell people how great you are. Humility is when you're willing to wait for other people to tell you how great you are.

Just think about the kids in your class who you really like. I'm not talking about the popular kids who you may or may not like. I'm talking about the kids you really like. I'll bet those kids you like are not the ones who go around bragging about themselves. I bet the kids you like are humble. I bet they ask how you're doing before they tell you how they're doing. I bet they help you before they ask you to help them. Humility is not just a good thing if you are a golfer. Humility is a good thing if you are anyone, anywhere, at any time.

Humble people are comfortable in their own skin. This saying seems funny, because how could you *not* be comfortable in your own skin? How could you try to jump out of your own skin? What it means is that you know who you are. It means that you understand what you are good at and you don't brag about it, and you understand what you are not good at and you try to get better.

When your parents ask you, "Just who do you think you are?" they're asking you why you're not comfortable in your own skin. And that question is not silly at all.

28

You may think that the biggest difference between you and your parents is that they get to drive a car and you don't. Really, the biggest difference is that they think life is too short, and you think life is too long. "Life's too short for this!" is one of the most mysterious sayings in the language of Parent. I'm sure that when you first hear it, you'll be as confused as I was when I first heard it. Let me try to translate for you.

I know that some days you must feel like your life is just one long wait in the dentist's office, waiting to get drilled. You sit through classes that are so boring you want to pull out your hair. You're always waiting for someone to take you somewhere and then when you get there, you usually have to wait for your friend to get there, and then when you're done, you have to wait for someone to pick you up. You're always told that you can't do this or that until you grow up, and every morning when you look at yourself in the mirror, you're still not grown up. The days when you can control your life seem to be far, far away.

So one day, you come home from school and you accidentally track mud all over the house or bump into and break some goofy statue of two angels playing harps (which you never liked but was given to your mom by her favorite aunt) and your mom freaks out. Then *you* freak out because she's getting so upset about such a dumb little accident, and before you know it you're both screaming at each other. It's times like these when a parent is likely to end the screaming by screaming, "Life's too short for this!" (as you get sent to your room even though you really had no idea what she was screaming about).

What your mom was saying is something like this: "Why do we have to do this? Why can't you be more thoughtful and more careful, and why can't I just realize that what you did was an accident and not done to make me crazy? I love you too much to argue with you anymore. None of this will matter in a few years or even in a few minutes. This arguing is so lame, so stupid, and most of all, it wastes time that should be spent living. I don't want to fight with you. I only want you to do the right thing and slow down and realize that some day you're going to wish you had back all the time you wasted yelling at me and sitting grounded in your room. Life is too short for this."

So, for a great life, whenever you get crazed or upset about how your parents or your teachers or your coaches or your friends are treating you, just practice saying over and over again, "It just doesn't matter. . . . It just doesn't matter." Most of the time you'll be right, and when it does matter, the people who are filling your life with their love will tell you. Life is just too short to sweat the small stuff. After all, you don't want to miss out on the really great big stuff.

29

Someday you'll laugh about this!

Have you ever been hit in the face with a pie? Probably not, but someday it will probably happen to you. Somebody will hit you with a pie, and everybody will laugh. As for you, you have a choice about what to do underneath that pie. You can laugh it off, or you can smack the pie thrower with a pie of your own. The best idea is to laugh it off.

Laughing is the only medicine you can take that doesn't taste awful. Laughter helps keep things real and helps you let go of anger, embarrassment, jealousy, or other bad feelings you have when you get all worked up about something. That's why "Someday you'll laugh about this" is almost always the right thing for a parent to say to help you let go of embarrassing moments in your life.

Sometimes the pie-in-the-face moments that you have to laugh off have no actual pie in them. If you didn't make the debate team or get the lead in the school play or make the cheerleading squad or the kick line, or if you didn't get invited to a party you really wanted to go to, or if you went to a party wearing the wrong clothes, or if your pants fell down at school, you might be so down that you feel your life is over. Of course your life isn't over. In fact, your life is just beginning, and laughing about it helps you remember that none of that stuff really matters in the long run. If you can't laugh on your own, somebody who loves you might

say to you, "Someday you'll laugh about this!" And even after they give you this good advice, if you're still too upset to laugh today, that's okay. Maybe you can laugh about it some other day. It's never too late to laugh.

You've probably heard a popular variation of this saying: time heals all wounds. It might be annoying to hear that, too, but you know it's true: How many cuts and scrapes did you get as a kid that healed right over and that you forgot all about until the scab fell off? A scab falling off shows that your body is ready to move on (so please try not to ever pick off a scab before it's ready to fall off — let it fall off by itself, for goodness' sake!). Laughing at your little hurts shows you are ready to move on, too.

Life is a long journey, and one of the best lessons you can learn is how to laugh along the way. The hardest people to live with are people who are serious about everything. They don't make life any fun, and if you can't have fun, what's the point? Laughing not only cheers you up, it cheers up the people around you. Some people think that laughing can even make your body healthier and help you live longer! How's that for a good reason to laugh?

So, try to think of the embarrassing moments in your

life as nothing but a banana-cream pie that hit you right in the face. How sad can you really get about having to lick yummy whipped cream off your nose and fingers? Life is sometimes just goofy and weird, so keep your sense of humor and try to enjoy the pie.

30

Winning is good; being popular is good; and succeeding at something you tried hard to do is good. But having people who are proud of you is the best of all.

You can win because your opponent was terrible; you can be popular just because you're pretty or handsome; and you can succeed because you're just naturally good at something but didn't have to work hard at it. People can like you for silly reasons, like the fact that your parents are friends with their parents, that you're good at sports, or that your family has lots of money.

But people can't be *proud* of you for silly reasons. They're proud of you because you made a hard but good choice. They're proud of you because you helped somebody who needed help. They're proud of you because you did the right thing, even if it cost you. They're proud of you because you worked really hard and made sacrifices to get to an important goal. For people to be proud of you, you always have to have accomplished something good.

This is why it feels so good when your parent or teacher or coach or friend tells you, "I'm so proud of you!" They're telling you that you're growing up to be a great person and that you're making good choices. When people are proud of you, it means that they see the deep parts of you that make you good, and not just the surface parts of you that make you popular.

It's almost always hard to do the right thing and almost always easy to do the popular thing, but doing the right thing is better. Over time, people who make good choices have better friends than people who just want to be liked. If your friends are doing dangerous things that might hurt them or other people — like eating way too many Twinkies, or throwing pencils, or smoking cigarettes — you can try to stop them. Even if that means telling some adult you trust, and even if that means losing the friendship; it's the right thing to do. It's the popular thing to just do nothing.

Like is just for now. Proud is forever. If you just want to be liked, you might do anything that will make you liked, but if you want to be good, there are certain things you just won't do no matter what it costs you. When somebody tells you that they like you, they could change their mind a minute later, but when they tell you that they're proud of you, it's a deep feeling that's hard to change.

"I'm so proud of you" is sometimes another way to say "I love you." Pride and love can go together like peanut butter and chocolate or like strawberries and shortcake (with whipped cream, of course!), as long as it's not the kind of pride that's directed at yourself and that makes you feel you're better than others. There are many different words that add up to "I love you." "I'm so proud of you," "Good job," "Nice going," and even "You da man!" can all be ways that your parents tell you that they're proud of

you and that they love you. In fact, "I'm proud of you" can be said without a single word. A big smile, a hug, a nod of the head, and a smile can all mean the same thing.

For some people words of love just don't come out easily. Some parents, especially dads, can have a hard time saying the words "I love you." They DO love you, though, with all their heart, but for some reason it's easier for them to say they're proud of you. You can learn how to translate their hugs and their smiles and their pats on the back (and even the tears they wipe away really fast) into the "I love you." The words don't matter all that much, as long as you know what they *really* mean.

31

This book has been filled with sayings written in the language called Parent that you're told all the time but might not understand all the time because you don't speak the language. At least, you didn't speak Parent until now!

I wanted the last chapter of this book to be a saying NOBODY is told all the time. This is a very special saying that comes from a very special story. It's a Native American story from the Cherokee nation, but like all great stories it has meaning for all people no matter what their tribe happens to be. Here is the story.

An old Cherokee chief took his grandchildren into the forest and sat them down and said to them, "A fight is going on inside me. This is a terrible fight and it is a fight between two wolves. One wolf is the wolf of fear, anger, arrogance, and greed. The other wolf is the wolf of courage, kindness, humility, and love." The children were very quiet and listening to their grandfather with both their ears as he then said to them, "This same fight between the two wolves that is going on inside of me is also going on inside of you, and inside of every person." They thought about it for a minute and then one child asked the chief, "Grandfather, which wolf will win the fight?" He said quietly, "The one you feed."

What this story means to me is what this book means to me. We all have two choices in our lives. We can do the right thing (and feed the good wolf) or we can do the wrong thing (and feed the bad wolf). Mostly, we know which wolf is which, but not always, and that's why the people who love you tell you things over and over again. They want you to make the right choices in your life. They want you to feed the right wolf, because the wolf you feed is the wolf that will win!

When you understand this, you won't get upset about the things parents tell you in the language of Parent — no matter how many times they say them. In fact, someday you may even thank them for speaking Parent to you. It's the way they show love; it's the way we learn; and ultimately, it's the way we make sure the good wolf wins in the end.